LAUGH OUT LOUD

I RUFF JOKES

I don't!

By Jeffrey Burton

LITTLE SIMON
New York London Toronto Sydney New Delhi

LITTLE SIMON
An imprint of Simon & Schuster Children's Publishing Division
1230 Avenue of the Americas, New York, New York 10020
First Little Simon edition September 2017

For information about special discounts for bulk purchases, please contact Simon & Schuster Special Sales at 1-866-506-1949 or business@simonandschuster.com.
The Simon & Schuster Speakers Bureau can bring authors to your live event. For more information or to book an event contact the Simon & Schuster Speakers Bureau at 1-866-248-3049 or visit our website at www.simonspeakers.com.
Designed by Brittany Naundorff
Manufactured in China 0617 QUL
10 9 8 7 6 5 4 3 2 1
ISBN 978-1-5344-0029-0
ISBN 978-1-5344-0030-6 (eBook)

Welcome and get ready to **LAUGH OUT LOUD** with this **Animal Meme Joke Book** that's out to prove once and for all that wildlife are the funniest critters on earth.

Before you start, here are some helpful tips to make this book even funnier:

- give each animal its own special voice
- give each joke its own special delivery
- make sure you share the best jokes with your friends
- and don't be afraid to make up your own jokes, too!

Hey! I know a great knock-knock joke. You start.

What if I'm just a cat, and you're just an unlucky person?

FINE! IF YOU'RE GOING TO BE THAT WAY,

I'M TAKING MY TOY
AND GOING HOME.

NUTS?

NUTS!

NUTS?

This hat looked bigger
in the store...

But he started it!

WHEN YOUR DAD EATS
THE LAST COOKIE.

OH MEOW GOSH, THE BALL HAS A

BELL INSIDE!

BAD
SELFIE.

I'm about to
UNLOCK
THE NEXT
HAMSTER LEVEL!

You're eating a stick, Jimmy.
A stick.

WELL, THIS IS ANOTHER FINE MESS YOU'VE GOTTEN YOURSELF INTO, NIBBLES.

OUT OF THE WAY!!!

Hi, I'm Sweetums.

I like eating scraps off the floor and chewing on dirty socks.

For the last time, kid,
I don't like carrots.

The secret password is . . .

doodles.

NO, REALLY. TELL MORE CAT JOKES. I LOVE CAT JOKES.

We're out of tea.

I BELIEVE THE WORD YOU'RE LOOKING FOR IS **ADORABLE.**

WHEN YOU'RE AT SCHOOL
AND YOU SEE OTHER KIDS OUTSIDE.

CAT,

CATTER,

CATTEST.

What do you MEAN
you SAVED OVER
my game?!

Here comes Hamster Claus.

Here comes Hamster Claus.

Right down Hamster Claus Lane.

SMILE!!

This is my smile.

THIS JACKET IS SO FLUFFY!
I CAN'T WAIT TO
SHRED IT!

You're so loud!
Use your
indoor voice.

THIS IS MY
INDOOR
VOICE!

WAIT—HUMANS DO
WHAT WITH THIS?

ABOUT THAT MODELING CAREER . . .

BAD SELFIE.

One is the loneliest number . . .

I've done the math.

ME?
GET THE BALL?
UH, NO.

When kids go to school and I'm like, don't mind me, I'm just gonna play with your toys all day.

We meet again, Mr. Duck.

WHEN YOU
GET THE JOKE
15 MINUTES
LATER.

When Ralphy tries to look happy,

but he knows your pizza is better than his dog food.

THE MAGIC CAT WILL
SEE YOU NOW.

SOCIAL MEOW-DIA

Want bonus
homework?

NEVER CHALLENGE THIS GUY TO A PUSH-UP BATTLE.

DOGS RULE!
(WINK)

Who has an underwater camera and is about to be my lunch?

This guy.

Can you believe this weather?

Excuse me,

do you know where the cat aisle is?

OH
GREAT.
I'M STUCK.

Moo!

Moo!

I told you, I’m not singing.

I've come from the future to warn you . . .
WE'RE OUT OF DOG FOOD.

Never chase your tail. You'll look like a fool.
But if a red dot appears, you must catch it at all costs.

Quit showing off, yoga master.

AS A MATTER OF
FACT, I WAS
RAISED IN THE WOODS.

MEANWHILE,
AT THE CAT
OLYMPICS . . .

Why is the whole world
upside down?

MOBILE HOME.

Mittens dares you

to wash your hands.

NO, I MEAN, IT LOOKS GOOD . . .

ON YOU.

Who likes eating trash?

Is it my turn to drive?

When mom insists you go to the school dance.

No one
can see me
because I'm
camel-flaged.

I heard you wanted to **PLAY!**

Oh . . .
you wanted some,
too?

'Twas I who stole the COOKIES from the COOKIE JAR!

when you see your parents

KISS.

SOMETHING SMELLS FUNNY.

NEXT STOP: ADVENTURE!

When you think there's a **ghost** behind you.

MONKEY FACT:

Anyone who smiles this much

has a secret. *A deep, dark secret.*

THE CAT KNOWS WHEN IT'S
TIME TO WAKE UP, HUMAN.

Well, the password's not my name . . .

Cat-tastic Dance Party!

Someone broke

kitty ballerina.

I GIVE UP.

Did you hear the one about the frog?

He croaked!

YOU DONE IN THE BATHROOM YET?

Just another day
at the beach.

THE LEMUR KNOWS WHAT YOU DID.

ME-ME-ME-ME-OOOWWWWWW!!!

The dirt's fine. Why don't you come in?

SEAFOOD?
WHERE?!

WAIT, THE BANANAS WERE FOR EVERYONE?

Horse hats optional.

the square root of cute and fluffy is animals in glasses.

Oh really, Mom? Tell me more about how much you *loved* homework when you were a kid.

My face when people miss me in dodgeball.

I'M READY FOR THE MARCH OF THE PENGUINS.

Hmmm, the stock market is going **bananas.**

The lifeguard is

on duty.

Hey, that cloud looks like a mouse!

Please don't ask for an omelette. Please don't ask for an omelette.

Is this a toy
or is it a
TRAP?

THIS WAS A BAD IDEA.

When
your present
is smaller
than what
you asked for.

MEET THE DREADED PARROT BLUEBIRD, SCOURGE OF THE ANIMAL ENCLOSURE AT THE ZOO.

We demand equal dinner rights.

Goo-goo, gah-gah.

Pardon me.
Might you spare a

SMIDGE OF
CHEESE?

WHEN YOU FORGET YOUR LINES IN THE SCHOOL PLAY.

We're going to the
future, Marty.

what was in that snail I ate?

WAITING FOR DAD TO PUT DOWN THE TV REMOTE.

MADE OF CUTE NIGHTMARES.

How dare you steal
from my litter box!

And birdseed. Don't forget to add birdseed to the list!

But I love riding my tiny bike!
TRAIL

I KNOW YOU DON'T LIKE ME SCRATCHING THE SOFA.
I JUST DON'T CARE.

Welcome to the

CONE OF SHAME.

Your face after someone says,
"TRY IT. YOU'LL LIKE IT."

And then I said, I don't.
I don't want a cracker.

One time I found
a rock that looked
exactly like me.
I named him Rocky.

CAT REALIZES THAT SHE
IS ALONE IN THE HOUSE.

The moment before your friend scares you to death.

WHEN YOUR LITTLE SISTER
TRIES TO TELL A JOKE.

This was a
bad idea.

Here's the problem:
My finger was in
your ear!

I've come to
grant you
three wishes–
no more,
no less.

Runner-up in the sadness contest.

Well, I never!

Sea lion

IS NOT

impressed.

Reading is

groovy, baby.

But so is walking your dog.

CAT KARATE KICK!

KEE-YAH!

Change the channel, or I'm
PULLING THE PLUG!

EVERYBODY DO THE

HAMSTER SHAKE!

whoa, it worked.

Sorry, I don't have any yarn to spare.

That's okay. I brought my own.

PAWS OFF MY COOKiES.

WHEN DAD MAKES
PIZZA "HEALTHY."

WAZZZZZZZZZUP?!

THIS TASTES AWFUL!

ARE YOU . . .
LICKING MY BACK?
DON'T DO THAT.
THAT'S WEIRD.

Throw me the ball!
I'm open!
I'm open!!

WHAT ANIMALS DREAM ABOUT.

Carl, get your head down.
We're playing hide-and-seek!

OKAY, TREE, YOU WANNA FIGHT?!
PUT 'EM UP!

Is that allowed in soccer?

WOLFDOG KNOWS
WHAT YOU DID.

WHEN YOUR BROTHER GETS THE SAME TOY AS YOU.

OH!
Where are
we going?

Is that a cat in a cowboy hat?

MEOWDY, PARDNER.

MEANWHILE, AT THE CAT OLYMPICS . . .

NATURE SMELLS

SO NATURE-Y.

Don't worry. I goat your back.

You're wearing the wrong costume.

I got this.
I got this.

I don't got this.

Hey! Socks just busted through a brick wall.

THE MOMENT YOU GET TOO
BIG FOR YOUR BRITCHES.

Let's hear what Professor Barkley has to say.

Look into my eyes.
You are under my doggy spell.

LEVITATE POWER!

WHEN YOUR SISTER ALSO
GETS TO STAY UP LATE.

HUMANS CONTROL THE TOYS?!

this little monkey toe went to the market . . .

Hello. So, do you

HANG AROUND HERE

often?

MAXIN' and Relaxin'

Hey!
You found me!

weirdest dude in school.

Can you help me put on this h-a-a-a-a-t?

DON'T CHANGE THE STATION WHEN MY SONG IS ON.

WHEN YOU TELL YOUR FRIENDS YOU DON'T LIKE THEIR FAVORITE BOOK.

SPOT REALIZES HE'S BEEN CHASING
HIS OWN TAIL ALL ALONG.

YOU
BROUGHT
CAKE?!

IT'S A CUPCAKE, CARL!
A SINGLE CUPCAKE!

FISH

DAREDEVIL

EVERY FRIDAY
AFTER SCHOOL,
KIDS BE LIKE

BEHOLD!
I am Lord Commander Cat!

NOT IMPRESSED.

Hot dogs

with

horseradish?

GROSS!

Mouse secret:
I took all the
bad selfie
pictures.

MIND. BLOWN.